The Gift of Inner Peace

THE GIFT OF INNER PEACE

Inspirational Writings by James Allen, Author of *As a Man Thinketh*

Edited by Marianne Wilson

♔

HALLMARK EDITIONS

CONTENTS

The Gift of Inner Peace

Introduction

James Allen's inspiring beliefs have influenced millions of English-speaking people everywhere. He lived as he believed — quietly devoted to the hope of a better, happier life.

James Allen was born in 1864 in Leicester, a county in Central England northeast of Birmingham. In 1879, a family financial crisis forced him to leave school. He was fifteen. From that time until 1902, Allen worked as an administrative assistant to several British manufacturers. Then, just nine years before his death, he decided to devote his life to writing. In the brief last years of his life, Allen wrote nineteen books, a rich outpouring of inspiration that would guide later generations. Allen dedicated himself to finding inner peace and happiness. He knew it existed in the depths of every man. It was there just for the cultivating.

Soon after finishing his first book, *From Poverty to Power*, Allen and his wife Lily moved to Ilfracombe, on England's southwest coast. It was there that his inspirational classic *As a Man Thinketh* was written.

His life at Ilfracombe was ideal for reflection and quiet thought. The day began with a predawn walk up to the Cairn, a stony spot on the hillside overlooking his home and the sea. He would remain there for an hour in meditation. Then he would return to the house and spend the morning writing. The afternoons were devoted to gardening, a pastime he enjoyed. His evenings were spent in conversation with those who were interested in his work. It was an idyllic existence. "A man cannot be separated from his mind," Allen wrote. "His life cannot be separated from his thoughts. Mind, thought and life are as inseparable as light, radiance, and color....It follows that deliberately to change the thoughts is to change the man."

According to his wife, Allen "wrote when he had a message, and it became a message only when he had lived it in his own life, and knew that it was good."

He saw that if man will use his power of good, by thinking clearly and acting intelligently, perfection of personality is attainable. When we seek self-knowledge through reflection, we experience a kinship with nature and a reconciliation with our outer life. In summation he eloquently says, "This, then, is the secret of health — a pure heart and a well-ordered mind; this is the secret of success — an unfaltering faith, and a wisely directed purpose;...this is the secret of power."

The Secret of Success

And I may stand where health, success, and power
Await my coming, if, each fleeting hour,
I cling to love and patience; and abide
With stainlessness; and never step aside
From high integrity; so shall I see
At last the land of immortality.

Right Beginnings

Life is full of beginnings. They occur every day and every hour to every person. Most beginnings are small and appear trivial and insignificant, but in reality they are the most important things in life.

See how in the material world everything proceeds from small beginnings. The mightiest river is at first a rivulet over which the grasshopper could leap; the great flood commences with a few drops of rain; the sturdy oak, that has endured the storms of a thousand winters, was once an acorn.

Consider how in the spiritual world the greatest things proceed from smallest beginnings. A light fancy may be the inception of a wonderful invention or an immortal work of art; a spoken sentence may turn the tide of history; a pure thought entertained may lead to the exercise of a worldwide regenerative power....

There are right beginnings and wrong beginnings, followed by effects of like nature. You can, by careful thought, avoid wrong beginnings and make right beginnings, and so escape evil results and enjoy good results....

Loving, gentle, kind, unselfish, and pure thoughts are right beginnings, leading to blissful results. This is so simple, so plain, so absolutely true; and yet how neglected, how evaded, and how little understood!

Your whole life is a series of effects, having their cause in thought — in your own thought. All conduct is made and molded by thought; all deeds, good or bad, are thoughts made visible.

The Importance of Sincerity

In the Confucian code of morals sincerity is one of the "Five Great Virtues," and Confucius thus speaks of it: "It is sincerity which places a crown upon our lives .... There can be no self-respect without it, and this is why the superior man must be guarded in his hours of solitude."...

Thus the sincere man does not do or say that which he would be ashamed of were it brought to light. His uprightness of spirit enables him to walk upright and confident among his fellow-men. His presence is a strong protection, and his words are direct and powerful because they are true. Whatever may be his work, it prospers. Though he may not always please the ears of men, he wins their hearts; they rely on him, trust and honor him.

Strength Is the Basis

Strength is the firm basis on which is built the temple of the Triumphant Life. Without a central motive and fixed resolve, your life will be a poor, weak, drifting, unstable thing. *Let the act of the moment be governed by the deep abiding purpose of the heart.* You will act differently at different times, but the act will not be wrong if the heart is right. You may fall and go astray at times, especially under great stress, but you will quickly regain yourself, and will grow wiser and stronger thereby so long as you guide yourself by the moral compass within....

Err on the side of strength rather than weakness. The measures you adopt may not be the best, but if they are the best you know, then your plain duty is to carry them out; by so doing you will discover the better way, if you are anxious for progress, and are willing to learn....

Rise up in your divine strength, and spurn from your mind and life all meanness and weakness. Do not live the false life of a puling slave, but live the true life of a conquering master.

Fitted for Conquest

He is truly wise who, in the midst of his worldly duties, is always calm, always gentle, always patient; who accepts things as they are, and does not wish and grieve, desire and regret. These things belong to the divinely conscious state, the dominion of Truth, and are indications of enlightenment, strength, and mastery....

Man is fitted for conquest, but the conquest of territory will not avail; he must resort to the conquest of self. The conquest of territory renders man a temporal ruler, but the conquest of self makes him an eternal conqueror.

Man is destined for mastery; not the mastery of his fellow men by force, but the mastery of his own nature by self-control. The mastery of his fellow men by force is the crown of egotism, but the mastery of self by self-control is the crown of humility....He is the calm spectator, no longer the helpless tool of events....He perceives the course of things with a glad and peaceful heart; a divine conqueror, master of life and death.

The Ultimate Triumph

He only finds peace who conquers himself, who strives, day by day, after greater self-possession, greater self-control, greater calmness of mind. *One can only be a joy to himself and a blessing to others in the measure that he has command of himself; and such self-command is gained only by persistent practice.* A man must conquer his weaknesses by daily effort; he must understand them and study how to eliminate them from his character; and if he continues to strive, not giving way, he will gradually become victorious; and each little victory gained (though there is a sense in which no victory can be called *little*) will be so much more calmness acquired and added to his character as an eternal possession. He will thus make himself strong and capable and blessed, fit to perform his duties faultlessly, and to meet all events with an untroubled spirit....

The mind of the calm man is like the surface of a still lake; it reflects life and things of life truly. Whereas the troubled mind, like the troubled surface of a lake, gives back a distorted image of all things which fall upon it. Gazing into the serene depths within him, the self-conquered man sees a just reflection of the universe. He sees the Cosmic Perfection; sees the equity in his own lot;

14

even those things which are regarded by the world as unjust and grievous (and which formerly appeared so to him) are now known to be the effects of his own past deeds, and are therefore joyfully accepted as portions of the perfect whole. Thus his calmness remains with him with its illimitable fund of resource in joy and enlightenment....

Where the calm mind is, there is strength and rest, there is love and wisdom; there is one who has fought successfully innumerable battles against self, who, after long toil in secret against his own failings has triumphed at last.

The Life Triumphant

Courage, self-reliance, sincerity, generosity and kindness — these are the virtues which constitute a robust manhood; without them, a man is but clay in the hands of circumstances; a weak, wavering thing that cannot rise into the freedom and joy of a true life. Every young man should cultivate and foster these virtues, and as he succeeds in living them, will he prepare himself to achieve the Life Triumphant.

The Path to Inner Peace

And I may seek and find; I may achieve;
I may not claim, but, losing, may retrieve.
The law bends not for me, but I must bend
Unto the law, if I would reach the end
Of my afflictions, if I would restore
My soul to Light and Life, and weep no more.

The Gift of Inner Peace

The first principles in life are principles of conduct. To name them is easy. As mere words they are on all men's lips, but as fixed sources of action, admitting of no compromise, few have learned them....I will deal with five only of these principles. These five are among the simplest of the root principles of life, but they are those that come nearest to the everyday life, for they touch the artisan, the business man, the householder, the citizen, at every point. Not one of them can be dispensed with but at severe cost, and he who perfects himself in their application will rise superior to many of the troubles and failures of life, and will come into these springs and currents of thought which flow harmoniously toward the regions of enduring success. First among these principles is-

DUTY. A much-hackneyed word, I know, but it contains a rare jewel for him who will seek it by assiduous application. The man who is continually instructing others, gratis, how to manage their affairs, is the one who most mismanages his own.

Duty also means undivided attention to the matter in hand, intelligent concentration of the mind on the work to be done; it includes all that

is meant by thoroughness, exactness, and efficiency. The details of duties differ with individuals, and each man should know his own duty better than he knows his neighbor's, and better than his neighbor knows his; but although the working details differ, the principle is always the same. Who has mastered the demands of duty?

HONESTY is the next principle. It means not cheating or overcharging another. It involves the absence of all trickery, lying and deception by word, look or gesture. It includes sincerity, the saying what you mean, and the meaning what you say. It scorns cringing policy and shining compliment. It builds up good reputations, and good reputations build up good business, and bright joy accompanies well-earned success. Who has scaled the heights of Honesty?

ECONOMY is the third principle. The conservation of one's financial resources is merely the vestibule leading toward the more spacious chambers of true economy. It means, as well, the husbanding of one's physical vitality and mental resources. It demands the conservation of energy by the avoidance of enervating self-indulgences and sensual habits. It holds for its follower, strength, endurance, vigilance, and capacity to achieve. It bestows great power on him who learns it well. Who has realized in all its force the supreme strength of Economy?

LIBERALITY follows economy. It is not opposed to it. Only the man of economy can afford to be generous. The spendthrift, whether in money, vitality, or mental energy, wastes so much on his own miserable pleasures as to have none left to bestow upon others. The giving of money is the smallest part of liberality. There is a giving of thoughts, and deeds, and sympathy, the bestowing of good-will, the being generous toward calumniators and opponents. It is a principle that begets a noble, far-reaching influence. It brings loving friends and staunch comrades, and is the foe of loneliness and despair. Who has measured the breadth of Liberality?

SELF-CONTROL is the last of these five principles, yet the most important. Its neglect is the cause of vast misery, innumerable failures, and tens of thousands of financial, physical, and mental wrecks. Show me the business man who loses his temper with a customer over some trivial matter, and I will show you a man who, by that condition of mind, is doomed to failure. If all men practiced even the initial stages of self-control, anger, with its consuming and destroying fire, would be unknown. The lessons of patience, purity, gentleness, kindness and steadfastness which are contained in the principle of self-control, are slowly learned by men, yet until they are truly learned, a man's character and success are uncertain and insecure. Where is the man who has perfected himself in self-control? Wherever he may be, he is a Master indeed.

The five principles are five practices, five avenues to achievement, and five sources of knowledge. It is an old saying and a good rule that "Practice makes perfect," and *he who would make his own the wisdom which is inherent in those principles, must not merely have them on his lips, they must be established in his heart.* To know them, and receive what they alone can bring, he must *do* them, and give them out in his actions....

If we observe right principles or causes, wrong effects cannot possibly accrue. If we pursue sound methods, no shoddy thread can find its way into the web of our life, no rotten brick enter into the building of our character to render it insecure; and if we do true actions, what but good results can come to pass; for to say that good causes can produce bad effects is to say that nettles can be reaped from a sowing of corn.

He who orders his life along the moral lines thus briefly enunciated, will attain to such a state of insight and equilibrium as to render him permanently happy and perennially glad;

all his efforts will be seasonably planted; all the issues of his life will be good, and though he may not become a millionaire — as indeed he will have no desire to become such — he will acquire the gift of peace, and true success will wait upon him as its commanding master.

As a Man Thinketh

Man is; and as he thinks, so he is. A perception and realization of these two facts alone — of man's being and thinking — lead into a vast avenue of knowledge which cannot stop short of the highest wisdom and perfection. One of the reasons why men do not become wise is that they occupy themselves with interminable speculations about a *soul* separate from themselves — that is, from their own mind — and so blind themselves to their actual nature and being. The supposition of a separate soul veils the eyes of man so that he does not see himself, does not know his mentality, is unaware of the nature of his thoughts without which he would have no conscious life.

Man's life is actual; his thoughts are actual; his life is actual. To occupy ourselves with the investigation of things that are, is the way of wisdom. Man considered as above, beyond, and separate from mind and thought, is speculative and not actual, and to occupy ourselves with the study of things that are not, is the way of folly.

Man cannot be separated from his mind; his life cannot be separated from his thoughts. Mind, thought, and life are as inseparable as light, radiance, and color, and are no more in need of another factor to elucidate them than are light, radiance, and color. The facts are all-sufficient, and contain within themselves the groundwork of all knowledge concerning them.

Man as mind is subject to change. He is not something "made" and finally completed, but has within him the capacity for progress. By the universal law of evolution he has become what he is, and is becoming that which he will be. His being is modified by every thought he thinks. Every experience affects his character. Every effort he makes changes his mentality. Herein is the secret of man's degradation, and also of his power and salvation if he but utilize this law of change in the right choice of thought.

To live is to think and act, and to think and act is to change. While man is ignorant of the nature of thought, he continues to change for better or worse; but, being acquainted with the nature of thought, he intelligently accelerates and directs the process of change, and only for the better....

Seeing that man is mind, that mind is composed of thought, and that thought is subject to change, it follows that deliberately to change the thought is to change the man.

A Life of Simplicity

A life of simplicity is simple in all its parts because the heart which governs it has become pure and strong....

The simple-hearted, the true-hearted, the virtuous and wise, are no longer troubled with doubts and fears about the future and the unknown and unknowable. They take their stand upon the duty of the hour, and on the known and the knowable. They do not barter away the actual for the hypothetical. They find in virtue an abiding security; they find in Truth an illuminating light which, while it reveals to them the true order of the facts of life, throws a halo of divine promise about the abyss of the unknown; and so they are at rest.

The Inner Life

The cause of all power, as of all weakness, is within: the secret of all happiness as of all misery is likewise within. There is no progress apart from unfoldment within, and no sure foothold of prosperity or peace except by orderly advancement in knowledge.

You say you are chained by circumstances; you cry out for better opportunities, for a wider scope, for improved physical conditions, and perhaps you inwardly curse the fate that binds you hand and foot. It is for you that I write; it is to you that I speak. Listen, and let my words burn themselves into your heart, for that which I say to you is truth: — *You may bring about that improved condition in your outward life which you desire, if you will unswervingly resolve to improve your inner life....*

There is no room for a complainer in a universe of law, and worry is soul-suicide. By your very attitude of mind you are strengthening the chains which bind you, and are drawing about you the darkness by which you are enveloped. Alter your outlook upon life, and your outward life will alter. Build yourself up in the faith and knowledge, and make yourself worthy of better surroundings and wider opportunities. Be sure, first of all, that you are making the best of what you have. Do not delude yourself into supposing that you can step into greater advantages whilst overlooking smaller ones, for if you could, the advantage would be impermanent and you would quickly fall back again in order to learn the lesson which you had neglected. As the child at school must master one standard before passing on to the next, so, before you can have that greater good which you so desire, must you faithfully employ that which you already possess...."If ye have faith, and doubt not, ye shall not only do this,...but if ye shall say unto this mountain, be thou removed and be thou cast into the sea, it shall be done."

A State of Blessedness

I know a lady who has entered into many blissful satisfactions, and recently a friend remarked to her, "Oh, how fortunate you are! You only have to wish for a thing, and it comes to you." And it did, indeed, appear so on the surface; but in reality all the blessedness that has entered into this woman's life is the direct outcome of the inward state of blessedness which she has, throughout life, been cultivating and training toward perfection. *Mere wishing brings nothing but disappointment; it is living that tells. The foolish wish and grumble; the wise work and wait.* And this woman had worked; worked without and within, but especially within upon heart and soul; and with the invisible hands of the spirit she had built up, with the precious stones of faith, hope, joy, devotion, and love, a fair temple of light, whose glorifying radiance was ever round about her. It beamed in her eye; it shone through her countenance; it vibrated in her voice; and all who came into her presence felt its captivating spell.

And as with her, so with you. Your success, your failure, your influence, your whole life you carry about with you, for your dominant trends of thought are the determining factors in your destiny. Send forth loving, stainless, and happy thoughts, and blessings will fall into your hands, and your table will be spread with the cloth of peace.

Little Gems of Wisdom

All strength and wisdom and
power and knowledge a
man will find within himself.

Be true to others, and others will be true to you ....If you have lost faith in human nature, discover where you have gone wrong yourself.

———◆•◆•◆———

The greatest blessedness comes to him who infuses into his mind the purest and noblest thoughts.

———◆•◆•◆———

Out of a hollow vessel nothing but the sound of hollowness can come; and from insincerity nothing but empty words can proceed.

———◆•◆•◆———

Deliberate beforehand, but in the time for action do not hesitate.

———◆•◆•◆———

Every moment you are sending forth from you the influence which will make or mar your life. Let your heart grow large and loving and unselfish, and great and lasting will be your influence and success.

Man has no enemy but self, no darkness but ignorance, no suffering but that which springs from the insubordinate elements of his own nature.

———◆•◉•◆———

Be self-reliant, but let thy self-reliance be saintly and not selfish.

———◆•◉•◆———

The wisest men dispense with all hypotheses, and fall back on the simple practice of virtue.

———◆•◉•◆———

The presumptuousness of the small may, for a time, obscure the humility of the great, but it is at last swallowed up by it, as the noisy river is lost in the calm ocean.

———◆•◉•◆———

As the true man does not speak in praise of himself or his own work, so the man of humility, charity, and wisdom does not speak of his own sect as being superior to all others.

Wisdom cannot be found in books or travel, in learning or philosophy, it is acquired by practice only.

There is no distinction between the pious Christian and the pious Buddhist. Purity of heart... and the love of Truth are the same in the Buddhist as the Christian.

The strong, calm man is always loved and revered.

Men differ about that which is unreal, not that which is real; they fight over error, and not over Truth.

We cannot realize the stately splendor of Truth while playing with the gaudy and attractive toys of pretty hypotheses. Truth is not an opinion, nor can any opinion enlarge or adorn it.

Duties which are irksome to the ungoverned, are things of joy to the calm man; indeed, in the calm life, the word "duty" receives a new meaning; it is no longer opposed to happiness, but it is one with happiness.

―――――◆・◉・◆―――――

Great is the need of sympathy. Great is the need of love.

―――――◆・◉・◆―――――

Simplicity works untrammelled, and becomes greatness and power.

―――――◆・◉・◆―――――

Spiritual achievements are the consummation of holy aspirations.

―――――◆・◉・◆―――――

Men do not attract that which they want, but that which they are.

―――――◆・◉・◆―――――

A creed will not bear a man up in the hour of temptation; he must possess the inward Knowledge which slays temptation.

How insignificant money-seeking looks in comparison with a happy life.

———————◆•◆•◆———————

The tempter is like a coward, he only creeps in at weak and unguarded points.

———————◆•◆•◆———————

Temptation accompanies weakness and defeat, but a man is destined for strength and victory.

———————◆•◆•◆———————

You may learn of another, but you must accomplish for yourself. Put away all external props, and rely upon the Truth within you.

———————◆•◆•◆———————

In the ocean of life the isles of blessedness are smiling, and the sunny shore of your ideal awaits your coming....In the ship of your soul reclines the commanding master. He does but sleep; wake him.

Pleasure has its place, and in its place it is good; but as an end, as a refuge, it affords no shelter.

———◆·◆·◆———

This…is the secret of health — a pure heart and a well-ordered mind; this is the secret of success — an unfaltering faith, and a wisely directed purpose.

———◆·◆·◆———

Creeds must be, and he who performs faithfully his duty in his particular creed, not interfering with or condemning his neighbor in the performance of his duty, is bringing the world nearer to perfection and peace.

———◆·◆·◆———

Aspiration can carry a man into heaven, but to remain there he must learn to conform his entire mind to heavenly conditions.

———◆·◆·◆———

A man must know himself if he is to know truth.

The Way to Wisdom

Not mine the arrogant and selfish claim
To all good things; be mine the lowly aim
To seek and find, to know and comprehend,
And wisdom-ward all holy footsteps wend.
Nothing is mine to claim or to command,
But all is mine to know and understand.

To Live in Love

To transmute everything into Happiness and Joy, this is supremely the work and duty of the Heavenly minded man. To reduce everything to wretchedness and deprivation is the process which the world-minded unconsciously pursue. *To live in Love is to work in Joy. Love is the magic that transforms all things into power and beauty.* It brings plenty out of poverty, power out of weakness, loveliness out of deformity, sweetness out of bitterness, light out of darkness, and produces all blissful conditions out of its own substantial but indefinable essence.

He who loves can never want. The universe belongs to Goodness, and it therefore belongs to the good man. It can be possessed by all without stint or shrinking, for Goodness, and the abundance of Goodness (material, mental, and spiritual abundance), is inexhaustible. Think lovingly, speak lovingly, act lovingly, and your every need shall be supplied; you shall not walk in desert places,...no danger shall overtake you.

Love sees with faultless vision, judges true judgment, acts in wisdom. Look through the eyes of Love, and you shall see everywhere the Beautiful and True; judge with the mind of Love, and you shall not err, shall wake no wail of sorrow; act in the spirit of Love, and you shall strike undying harmonies upon the Harp of Life.

As Ye Sow, So Shall Ye Reap

Man attains in the measure that he aspires. His longing to be is the gauge of what he can be. To fix the mind is to fore-ordain the achievement. *As man can experience and know all low things, so he can experience and know all high things.* As he has become human, so he can become divine. The turning of the mind in high and divine directions is the sole and needful task.

What is impurity but the impure thoughts of the thinker? What is purity but the pure thoughts of the thinker? One man does not do the thinking of another. Each man is pure or impure of himself alone.

If a man thinks, "It is through others, or circumstances, or heredity that I am impure," how can he hope to overcome his errors?...

When a man fully perceives that his errors and impurities are his own, that they are generated and fostered by himself, that he alone is responsible for them, then he will aspire to overcome them, the way of attainment will be opened up to him.

The Permanent and Essential

In a sweet, methodical, well-managed house... discomfort and care are not allowed to accumulate; or should they have accumulated, they are gathered up and consigned to the fire and the dust bin, when it is decided to cleanse and restore the house, and give it light, comfort and freedom.

In like manner men hoard up in their minds mental rubbish and lumber, and cling tenaciously to it, and fear its loss....Simplicity consists in being rid of painful confusion of desires and superfluity of opinions, and adhering only to that which is permanent and essential.

And what is permanent in life? What is essential? Virtue alone is permanent; character is essential. So simple is life when it is freed from all superfluities and rightly understood and lived, that it can be reduced to a few unmistakable, easy-to-be-understood, though hard-to-practice principles; and all great minds have so simplified life. Buddha reduced it to eight virtues, in the practice of which he declared that men would acquire perfect enlightenment; and these eight virtues he reduced to one, which he called *Compassion*. Confucius taught that the perfection of knowledge was contained in five virtues, and these he expressed in one which he called *Reciprocity*, or *Sympathy*. Jesus reduced the whole of life to the principle of *Love*. Compassion, Sympathy, Love, these three are identical. How simple they are, too! yet I cannot find a man who fully understands the depths and heights of these virtues, for who so fully understood them would embody them in practice. He would be complete, perfect, divine. There would be nothing lacking in him of knowledge and virtue and wisdom. It is only when a man sets earnestly to work to order his life in accordance with the simple precepts of virtue, that he discovers what piles of mental rubbish he has hoarded up, and which he is now compelled to throw away. The exactions, too, which such a course of conduct makes upon his faith, endurance, patience, kindness, humility, reason, and strength of will, are, until the mind approaches the necessary condition of purity and simplicity, painful in their severity. The clearing-out process, whether of one's mind, home, or place of business, is not a light and easy one, but it ends in comfort and repose.

The Well-Governed Life

When mental energy is allowed to follow the line of least resistance, and to fall into easy channels, it is called weakness; when it is gathered, focused, and forced into upward and difficult directions, it becomes power; and this concentration of energy and acquisition of power is brought about by means of self-control.

In speaking of self-control, one is easily misunderstood. It should not be associated with a destructive repression, but with a constructive expression. The process is not one of death, but of life; it is a divine and masterly transmutation in which the weak is converted into the strong, the coarse into the fine, and the base into the noble; in which virtue takes the place of vice, and dark passion is lost in bright intellectuality.

The man who merely smothers up and hides away his real nature without any higher object in view than to create a good impression upon others concerning his character, is practicing hypocrisy, and not self-control. As the mechanic transmutes coal into gas, and water into steam, and then concentrates and utilizes the finer forces thus generated for the comfort and convenience of men, so the man who intelligently practices self-control transmutes his lower inclinations into the finer qualities of intelligence and morality to the increase of his own and the world's happiness.

The Highest Way

The Path of Wisdom is the highest way, the way in which all doubt and uncertainty are dispelled and knowledge and surety are realized....

Wisdom is "rejected of men" because it always comes right home to one's self in the form of wounding reproof, and the lower nature of man cannot bear to be reproved....

The Way of Wisdom is always open, is always ready to receive the tread of the pilgrim who has grown weary of the thorny and intricate ways of folly. No man is prevented from becoming wise but by himself; no man can acquire Wisdom but by his own exertions; and he who is prepared to be honest with himself, to measure the depths of his ignorance, to come face to face with his errors, to recognize and acknowledge his faults, and at once to set about the task of his own regeneration, such a man will find the way of Wisdom, walking which with humble and obedient feet, he will in due time come to the sweet City of Deliverance.

The Unfailing Wisdom

A man should be superior to his possessions, his body, his circumstances and surroundings, and the opinions of others and their attitudes toward him. Until he is this, he is not strong and steadfast. He should also rise superior to his own desires and opinions; and until he is this, he is not wise.

The man who identifies himself with his possessions will feel that all is lost when these are lost; he who regards himself as the outcome and the tool of circumstances will weakly fluctuate with every change in his outward condition; and great will be his unrest and pain who seeks to stand upon the approbation of others.

To detach oneself from every outward thing and to rest securely upon the inward Virtue, this is the Unfailing Wisdom. Having this Wisdom, a man will be the same whether in riches or poverty. The one cannot add to his strength, nor the other rob him of his serenity. Neither can riches defile him who has washed away all the inward defilement, nor the lack of them degrade him who has ceased to degrade the temple of his soul.

To refuse to be enslaved by any outward thing or happening, regarding all such things and happenings as for your use, for your education, this is Wisdom. To the wise all occurrences are *good*, and, having no eye for evil, they grow wiser every day. They utilize all things, and thus put all things under their feet. They see all their mistakes as soon as made, and accept them as lessons of intrinsic value, knowing that there are no mistakes in the Divine Order. They thus rapidly approach the Divine Perfection. They are moved by none, yet learn from all. They crave love from none, yet give love to all. To learn, and not to be shaken; to love where one is not loved; herein lies the strength which shall never fail a man.

The Way to Wisdom

The mass of humanity moves slowly along the evolutionary path urged by the blind impulse of its dominant thoughts as they are stimulated and called forth by external things; but the true thinker, the sage, travels swiftly and intelligently along a chosen path of his own. The multitudes, unenlightened concerning their spiritual nature, are the slaves of thought, but the sage is the master of thought. They follow blindly; he chooses intelligently. They obey the impulse of the moment, thinking of their immediate pleasure and happiness; he commands and subdues impulse, resting upon that which is permanently right. They, obeying blind impulse, violate the law of righteousness; he, conquering impulse, obeys the law of righteousness. The sage stands face to face with the facts of life. He knows the nature of thought. He understands and obeys the law of his being.

But the sorrow-burdened victim of blind impulse can open his mental eyes and see the true nature of things when he wishes to do so. The sage — intelligent, radiant, calm — and the fool — confused, darkened, disturbed — are one in essence, and are divided only by the nature of their thoughts; when the fool turns away from and abandons his foolish thoughts and chooses and adopts wise thoughts, lo! he becomes a sage.

Socrates saw the essential oneness of virtue and knowledge, and so every sage sees. Learning may aid and accompany wisdom, but it does not lead to it. *Only the choosing of wise thoughts, and necessarily, the doing of wise deeds, leads to wisdom. A man may be learned in the schools, but foolish in the school of life.* Not the committing of words to memory, but the establishing oneself in purer thoughts, nobler thinking, leads to the peace-giving revelations of true knowledge.

Folly and wisdom, ignorance and enlightenment, are not merely the result of thought, they are thought itself. Both cause and effect — effort and result — are contained in thought.

> *"All that we are is the result of what we*
> *have thought.*
> *It is founded on our thoughts; it is made up*
> *of our thoughts."*

Man is not a being possessing a soul, another self. He himself is soul. He himself is the thinker and doer, actor and knower. His composite mentality is himself. His spiritual nature is rounded by his sphere of thought. He it is that desires and sorrows, enjoys and suffers, loves and hates. The mind is not the instrument of a metaphysical, superhuman soul. Mind is soul; mind is being; mind is man.

Man can find himself. He can see himself as he is. When he is prepared to turn from the illusory and self-created world of hypothesis in which he wanders, and to stand face to face with actuality, then will he know himself as he is; moreover, he can picture himself as he would wish to be, and can create within him the new thinker, the new man; for every moment is the time of choice — and every hour is destiny.

The Eternal Light

Call him immortal, call him Truth and Light
And splendor of prophetic majesty
Who bideth thus amid the powers of night,
Clothed with the glory of divinity.

Truth — the Eternal Religion

The precepts of the Sermon on the Mount are to be found in all religions, and the life which those precepts demand was lived by all the Great Teachers and many of their disciples, for the Truth is a pure heart and a blameless life, and not a set of dogmas and opinions. *All religions teach purity of heart, holiness of life, compassion, love, and good-will; they teach the doing of good deeds and the giving up of selfishness and sin.* These things are not dogmas, theologies, and opinions, they are things to be done, to be practiced, to be lived. Men do not differ about these things, for they are the acknowledged verities in every sect. What, then, do they differ about? About their opinions, their speculations, their theologies....

All religions are the same in that they teach the same fundamental verities, but men, instead of practicing these verities, engage in opinions and speculations about things which are outside the range of knowledge and experience, and it is in defending and promulgating their own particular speculations that men become divided and engage in conflict with each other.

Condemnation is incipient persecution. The thought, "I am right and you are wrong," is a seed prolific of hatred. It was out of this seed that the Spanish Inquisition grew. He who would find the universal Truth must abandon egotism, must quench the hateful flames of condemnation, and, taking out of his heart the baneful thought, "All others are wrong," must think the illuminating thought, "It is I who am wrong," and having thus thought, he will cease from sin, and will live in love and good-will toward all, making no distinctions, engaging in no divisions, a peacemaker not a partisan. Thus living charitably disposed toward all, he will become one with all, and will comprehend the Universal Truth, the Eternal Religion; for while error refutes error and selfishness divides, Truth demonstrates Truth and Religion unifies.

All That We Are

What you are, so is your world. Everything in the universe is resolved into your own inward experience. It matters little what is without, for it is all a reflection of your own state of consciousness. It matters everything what you are within, for everything without will be mirrored and colored accordingly.

All that you positively know is contained in

your own experience; all that you ever will know must pass through the gateway of experience, and so become part of yourself.

Your own thoughts, desires, and aspirations comprise your world, and, to you, all that there is in the universe of beauty and joy and bliss, or of ugliness and sorrow and pain, is contained within yourself. *By your own thoughts you make or mar your life, your world, your universe. As you build within by the power of thought, so will your outward life and circumstances shape themselves accordingly.* Whatsoever you harbor in the inmost chambers of your heart will sooner or later by the inevitable law of reaction, shape itself in your outward life. The soul that is impure, sordid and selfish, is gravitating with unerring precision toward misfortune and catastrophe; the soul that is pure, unselfish, and noble, is gravitating with equal precision toward happiness and prosperity. Every soul attracts its own, and nothing can possibly come of it that does not belong to it. To realize this is to recognize the universality of Divine Law. The incidents of every human life, which both make and mar, are drawn to it by the quality and power of its own inner thought-life. Every soul is a complex combination of gathered experiences and thoughts, and the

body is but an improvised vehicle for its mani-
festation. What, therefore, your thoughts are,
that is your real self; and the world around, both
animate and inanimate, wears the aspect with
which your thoughts clothe it. "All that we are
is the result of what we have thought; it is
founded on our thoughts: it is made up of our
thoughts." Thus said Buddha, and it therefore
follows that if a man is happy, it is because he
dwells in happy thoughts; if miserable, because
he dwells in despondent and debilitating
thoughts. Whether one be fearful or fearless,
foolish or wise, troubled or serene, within that
soul lies the cause of its own state or states, and
never without.

A Salute to Self-Respect

*Be true to the dictates of your own conscience,
and respect all who do the same, even though
their conscience should lead them in a direction
the reverse of your own.* One of the most un-
manly tendencies is to pity another because he
chooses opinions or religion contrary to those of
one's self. Why pity a man because he is an Ag-
nostic, or an Atheist, or a Buddhist, or a Christian? Because he does not hold this opinion or

that belief? Such pity would be rightly named contempt. It is the office of pity to feel for the weak, the afflicted, and the helpless. Pity never says "I pity you"; it does kind deeds. It is super-ciliousness that professes pity for the strong, the self-reliant, for those who have the courage to mark out their own path and to walk it boldly. Why should he perforce hold my opinion or yours? If what I say and do appeal to his reason and conscience as right, then he will be one with me and will work hand in hand with me. But if my work be not his work, he is none the less a man. He has his duty, though it be not my duty. When I meet one who is self-respecting, and who dares to think for himself, I will salute him as a man, and not harbor in my heart a con-temptible pity for him, because, forsooth, he rejects my conclusions.

The True Spirit of Religion

Those who depart from the common track in matters of faith, and strike out independently in search of the Higher Life as distinguished from the letter of religious dogma, are apt to sink into a pitfall which awaits them at the first step, namely, the pitfall of *pride*. Attacking "creeds," and speaking contemptuously of the "orthodox" (as though orthodoxy were synonymous with evil) are not uncommon practices among those who fondly imagine they are in possession of greater spiritual light. Departure from orthodoxy does not by any means include departure from sin; indeed, it is not infrequently accompanied with increased bitterness and contempt. *Change of opinion is one thing, change of heart is quite another. To withdraw one's adherence from creeds is easy; to withdraw one's self from sin is more difficult.*

Hatred and pride, and not necessarily orthodoxy and conformity, are the things to be avoided. One's own sin, and not another man's creed, is the thing to be despised. The right-minded man cannot plume himself on being "broader" than others, or assume that he is on a "higher plane" than others, or think with pharisaical contempt of those who still cling to some form of letter worship which he has abandoned. Applying the words "narrow," "bigoted," and "selfish" to others, is not the indication of an enlightened mind. No person would wish these terms to be applied to himself, and he who is becoming truly religious, does not speak of others in words which would wound him were they directed toward himself....

Amid all the diversities of creeds there is the unifying power of undying and unalterable Love — and he who has Love has entered into sympathetic union with all.

Loving Repose

The right-thinker has discovered and acquired the right attitude of mind toward men and things — the attitude of a profound and loving repose. And this is not resignation, it is wisdom. It is not indifference, but watchful and penetrating insight. He has comprehended the facts of life; he sees things as they are. He does not overlook the particulars of life, but reads them in the light of cosmic law; sees them in their right relations as portions of the universal scheme. He sees that the universe is upheld by justice. He watches, but does not engage in, the petty quarrels and fleeting strifes of men. He cannot be a partisan. His sympathy is with all. He cannot favor one portion more than another. He knows that good will ultimately conquer in the world, as it has ...in individuals; that there is a sense in which good already conquers, for evil defeats itself.

The Freedom and Joy of Simplicity

"What," asked the learned man of the Buddhist saint who had acquired a wide reputation for sanctity and wisdom — "what is the most fundamental thing in Buddhism?" The saint replied, "The most fundamental thing in Buddhism is to cease from evil and to learn to do good." "I did not ask you," said the learned man, "to tell me what every child of three knows; I want you to tell me what is the most profound, the most subtle, the most important thing in Buddhism." "The most profound, the most subtle, the most important thing in Buddhism," said the saint, "is to cease from evil and to learn to do good. It is true that a child of three may know it, but grey haired old men fail to put it into practice." The commentator then goes on to say that the learned man did not want facts; he did not want Truth; he wanted to be given some subtle metaphysical speculation which would give rise to another speculation, and then to another and another, and so afford him an opportunity of bringing into play the wonderful intellect of which he was so proud.

A member of a philosophical school once proudly said to me, "Our system of metaphysics is the most perfect and complicated in the world." I discovered how complicated it was by becoming involved in it and then pursuing the process of extrication back to the facts of life, to simplicity and freedom. I have since learned how better to utilize my energy and occupy my time in the pursuit and practice of those virtues that are firm and sure, rather than to waste it in the spinning of the pretty but unsubstantial threads of metaphysical cobwebs.

But while discountenancing assumption and pride, and that vanity which mistakes its own hypothesis for reality, I set no premium on ignorance and stupidity. Learning is a good thing. As an end in itself, as a possession to be proud of, it is a dead thing; but as a means to the high ends of human progress and human good it becomes a living power. Accompanied with a lowly mind, it is a powerful instrument for good. The Buddhist saint was no less learned than his proud questioner, but he was more simple and wise. Even hypotheses will not lead us astray if they are perceived as mere hypotheses and are not confounded with facts. Yet the wisest men dispense with all hypotheses, and fall back on the simple practice of virtue. They thus become divine, and arrive at the acme of simplicity, enlightenment, and emancipation.

To arrive at the freedom and joy of simplicity,

one must not think less, he must think more;
only the thinking must be set to a high and use-
ful purpose, and must be concentrated upon the
facts and duties of life, instead of dissipated in
unprofitable theorizing.

Happy Endings

Life has many happy endings, because it has
much that is noble and pure and beautiful. Although there is much sin and ignorance in the
world, many tears, and much pain and sorrow,
there is also much purity and knowledge, many
smiles, and much healing and gladness. No pure
thought, no unselfish deed can fall short of its
felicitous result, and every such result is a happy
consummation.

A pleasant home is a happy ending; a success-
ful life is a happy ending; a task well and faithfully done is a happy ending; to be surrounded
by kind friends is a happy ending. A quarrel
put away, grudges wiped out, unkind words
confessed and forgiven, friend restored to friend
—all these are happy endings. To find that
which one has long and tediously sought; to be
restored from tears to gladness; to awaken in the
bright sunlight out of the painful nightmare of

sin; to strike...the Heavenly Way in life — these are, indeed, blessed consummations.

He who looks for, finds, and enters the by-ways which I have indicated will come to this one without seeking it, for his whole life will be filled with happy endings. He who begins right and continues right does not need to desire and search for felicitous results; they are already at hand; they follow as consequences: they are the certainties, the realities of life.

These are happy endings which belong solely to the material world; these are transient, and they pass away. There are happy endings which belong to the spiritual world; these are eternal, and they do not pass away. Sweet are companionships, pleasures, and material comforts, but they change and fade away. Sweeter still are Purity, Wisdom, and the knowledge of Truth, and these never change nor fade away. Wherever a man goes in this world he can take his worldly possessions with him; but soon he must part company with them, and if he stands upon these alone, deriving all his happiness from them, he will come to a spiritual ending of great emptiness and want. But he who has attained to the possession of spiritual things can never be deprived of his source of happiness: he will never have to part company with it, and wherever he goes in the whole universe he will carry his possessions with him. His spiritual end will be the fulness of joy.

Happy in the Eternal Happiness is he who has come to that Life from which the thought of self is abolished. Already, even now and in this life, he has entered the Kingdom of Heaven, Nirvana, Paradise, the New Jerusalem, the Olympus of Jupiter, the Valhalla of the Gods. He knows the Final Unity of Life, the Great Reality of which these fleeting and changing names are but feeble utterances. He is at rest on the bosom of the Infinite.

Sweet is the rest and deep the bliss of him who has freed his heart from its lusts and hatreds and dark desires; and he who, without any shadow of bitterness or selfishness resting upon him, and looking out upon the world with boundless compassion and love, can breathe, in his inmost heart, the blessing:

Peace unto all living things,

making no exceptions or distinctions — such a man has reached that happy ending which can never be taken away, for this is the perfection of life, the fulness of peace, the consummation of Perfect Blessedness.

Set in Patina
Printed on Hallmark
Eggshell Book Paper

Designed by Burton Huber